EYE TO EYE WITH DOGS

POODLES

Lynn M. Stone

Rourke
Publishing LLC
Vero Beach, Florida 32964

www.rourkepublishing.com

PHOTO CREDITS: All photos © Lynn M. Stone

Cover: *Although these dogs are often thought of as French, the first poodle-like dogs were used in Asia as herding dogs.*

Acknowledgments: For their help in the preparation of this book, the author thanks humans June Connelly, Greg Fay, Joanne Heritsch, John McGuire, Audrey Rose O'Keefe, and Nancy Olson; and canines Juno, Peaches, Zorro, and others.

Editor: Frank Sloan

Cover and page design by Nicola Stratford

Library of Congress Cataloging-in-Publication Data

Stone, Lynn M.
　　Poodles / Lynn M. Stone.
　　　　p. cm. — (Eye to eye with dogs)
　　Summary: A brief introduction to the physical characteristics, temperament, uses, and breeding history of the poodle.
　　Includes bibliographical references (p.).
　　ISBN 1-58952-330-X
　　1. Poodles—Juvenile literature. [1. Poodles. 2. Dogs.] I. Title.

SF429.P85 S69 2002
636.72'8—dc21   2002017839

Printed in the USA

MP/W

Table of Contents

Standard poodles are the original poodles and the largest poodle type.

The Poodle

Many people think poodles are fancy, fluffy little dogs from France. Actually, poodles are not always little, nor are they truly French!

Poodles come in three sizes: standard, miniature, and toy, the smallest variety. Miniature poodles and toys are quite small. But the standard poodle can weigh 65 pounds (29.5 kilograms). That's what many golden and Labrador retrievers weigh.

MINIATURE POODLE FACTS	
Weight:	26-30 pounds (12-14 kilograms)
Height:	11-15 inches (28-38 centimeters)
Country of Origin:	France
Life Span:	12-15 years

There's a poodle of a size for almost any home or dog lover. That's one reason poodles are among the most popular dogs in North America.

The popular, playful poodle comes in smaller packages than the standard.

A miniature poodle shows off one of the famous poodle clips.

The American Kennel Club (AKC) and Canadian Kennel Club (CKC) keep records of **purebred** dogs. In recent years, poodles ranked sixth in new **registrations** in the United States. They ranked fourth in Canada.

Poodles of the Past

The first poodle-like dogs probably came from Asia. There they were used largely to herd sheep and goats. By the 1400s they had been taken into Germany, Russia, France, and other European countries. The modern poodle is probably most like its German **ancestors.**

The modern poodle has borrowed some of its looks and behavior from its German poodle ancestors.

Even poodle pups show the breed's rough, curly coat.

Among poodle ancestors were many water-loving dogs with rough, curly coats. The English word poodle was borrowed from a German word, *pfudel*, which means "to splash." Its French name, *caniche*, means "duck dog."

The poodle became a special favorite in France. Wealthy French women often owned poodles. The poodle eventually became the national dog of France.

TOY POODLE FACTS
Weight: 14-16 pounds (6.5-7.5 kilograms)
Height: 8-10 inches (20-25 centimeters)
Country of Origin: France
Life Span: 12-15 years

Miniature and toy poodles were developed by dog **breeders** from standard poodles. Breeders used the smallest standards as mothers and fathers. Over many years, the breeders developed smaller and smaller poodles.

Poodles are kept largely as pets, not working dogs.

The poodle's special hairdo probably began when it was a working, water dog.

Poodles today are kept mostly as household pets. But poodles in the past were trained to guide, guard, retrieve ducks, and perform in circuses.

Clipping Poodles

The poodle's famous hair **clip** probably began during its water dog days. The coat was trimmed in places so that the dog could swim faster. But hair was left longer on the poodle's chest for warmth in the water.

The practice of leaving tufts of hair on the poodle's legs and tail probably began for circus shows. AKC dog shows today allow any of three different clips for adult poodles.

*A fluffy standard poodle pup wears the special puppy
clip of the breed.*

Poodles are easy to pick out from the dog crowd by their haircuts.

16

Looks

Poodles are one of the easiest dog **breeds** to pick out. Their coats are dense and curly wherever they're not shaved. The hair on poodle feet, for instance, is allowed to grow into tufts that look like snowballs. Poodle tails are **docked**, so they're short.

Poodles have slim, firm bodies from their hard-working ancestors. They have floppy ears and long, rather sharp **muzzles**.

Poodle Companions

Poodles are smart, playful, obedient, and friendly toward people. In fact, they need a great deal of human attention. Smaller poodles, especially, have lots of energy.

Poodles need plenty of human attention—some of it from the groomer.

This poodle sits while her master-musician plays.

Standard poodles need more exercise time than smaller poodles. Many standards, like their ancestors, love to swim and romp in woodlands.

Each dog of any breed has its own personality. But generally, standard poodles are calmer than their smaller cousins. All poodles are alert and quick to bark, so they make good watchdogs.

Poodle hair requires plenty of care with a brush. Poodles shed in an unusual way. Most shed hair is caught in their curly coat rather than falling to the floor.

STANDARD POODLE FACTS

Weight: 45-70 pounds
(20.5-30 kilograms)

Height: 15 inches or above
(38 centimeters
or above)

Country of Origin:
Germany, Central
Europe

Life Span: 10-13 years

Sitting on command, a standard poodle waits for a woodland romp.

A Note About Dogs

Puppies are cute and cuddly, but buying one should never be done without serious thought. Choosing the right breed of dog requires some homework. And remember that a dog will require more than love and great patience. It will require food, exercise, grooming, a warm, safe place to live, and medical care.

A dog can be your best friend, but you need to be its best friend, too. For more information about buying and owning a dog, contact the American Kennel Club at http://www.akc.org/index.cfm or the Canadian Kennel Club at http://www.ckc.ca/.

Glossary

ancestors (AN ses tuhrz) — those in the past from whom an animal has descended; direct relatives from the past

breeds (BREEDZ) — particular kinds of domestic animals within a larger group, such as the poodle breed within the dog group

breeders (BREE duhrz) — people who raise animals, such as dogs, and carefully choose the mothers and fathers for more dogs

clip (KLIP) — any particular hair style

docked (DOKT) — to have had an otherwise longer tail cut short

muzzles (MUZ uhlz) — the nose and jaws of animals; the snouts

purebred (PYOOR bred) — an animal of a single (pure) breed

registrations (rehj uh STRAY shunz) — official records of membership in a group

Index

Further Reading

Kallen, Stuart. *Poodles*. ABDO Publishing, 1996

Websites to Visit

Poodle Club of America at: http://www.poodleclubofamerica.org
Wonderful World of Poodles at:
http://www.geocities.com/Heartland/2826/

About the Author

Lynn Stone is the author of over 400 children's books. He is a talented natural history photographer as well. Lynn, a former teacher, travels worldwide to photograph wildlife in its natural habitat.